You Can't Go Back, Exactly

Books By
LOUIS DANIEL BRODSKY

Poetry
Trilogy: A Birth Cycle (1974)
Monday's Child (1975)
The Kingdom of Gewgaw (1976)
Point of Americas II (1976)
Preparing for Incarnations (1976)
La Preciosa (1977)
Stranded in the Land of Transients (1978)
The Uncelebrated Ceremony of Pants Factory Fatso (1978)
Birds in Passage (1980)
Résumé of a Scrapegoat (1980)
Mississippi Vistas (1983)
You Can't Go Back, Exactly (1988)
The Thorough Earth (1989)

Bibliography (Co-authored with Robert W. Hamblin)
Selections from the William Faulkner Collection of
    Louis Daniel Brodsky: A Descriptive Catalogue (1979)

Faulkner: A Comprehensive Guide to the Brodsky
    Collection:
        Volume I: The Biobibliography (1982)
        Volume II: The Letters (1984)
        Volume III: The De Gaulle Story (1984)
        Volume IV: Battle Cry (1985)
        Volume V: Manuscripts and Documents (1989)

Country Lawyer and Other Stories for the Screen by
    William Faulkner (1987)

Stallion Road: A Screenplay by William Faulkner (1989)

Biography
William Faulkner: Life Glimpses (1990)

You Can't
Go Back, Exactly

Poems by
Louis Daniel Brodsky

Timeless Press
Saint Louis, Missouri

First Edition, First Printing (August 1988)
Second Printing (October 1988)
Second Edition, First Printing (August 1989)

Timeless Press, Inc.
10411 Clayton Road
Saint Louis, Missouri 63131

Library of Congress Catalog Card Number: 89-50806

ISBN 1-877770-00-0
ISBN 1-877770-01-9 (tape)
ISBN 1-877770-02-7 (tape & pbk set)

Manufactured in the United States of America
Southeast Missouri State University

Cover photo by Jim Rosen

The author would like to express his gratitude to Darlene
Mathis-Eddy, poetry editor of Ball State University *Forum*,
for permission to reprint the following poems which first
appeared in its pages: "Tone Poem for Two Voices,"
"Accompanying My Son to Summer Camp," "Of Fishes
and Bears," "Morning's Companion," "Cabin by a Lake,"
"The Fishing Dock," "The Point."

Also, I would like to make special acknowledgement to
Linda Hermelin for her insightful editorial assistance; and
to Bruce F. Kawin, Will Fisher, Frank Sachs, and Arlene B.
Dowd for sensitive readings which enhanced specific poems
in this volume.

To

Muggs and Janet Lorber

&

Nardie and Sally Stein

whose belief in the nobility of camping,

compassion for and fascination with campers,

and steadfast devotion to

Camp Nebagamon for Boys

have endured sixty years

collectively,

this book is lovingly dedicated

There is a destiny that makes us brothers,
None goes his way alone:
All that we send into the lives of others
Comes back into our own.

I care not what his temples or his creeds,
One thing holds firm and fast:
That into his fateful heap of days and deeds
The Soul of a man is cast.

Edwin Markham

"Make a few good friends this summer, Mr. Boy!
Friends are the best companions your memories will
ever have."

Louis Daniel Brodsky in a letter
to his son Troika, 7/11/88.

CONTENTS

You Can't Go Back, Exactly

Children of All Ages

The Rec' Hall is a boy hive
Alive with buzzing, busy, dizzy voices.
And from the distance I hear another voice
Calling out behind my age:
"Face the facts, lad!
There's no disgrace in growing up,
Sowing seeds, leaving home,
Being on your own,
Unless you let the past
Impose rules on your future
By allowing the present
To glorify prior accomplishments."

Ah, boys! I see in you
What I must have been at ten:
Dreamy-eyed, ruddy chub-cheeks,
With the "husky" body of a tottering bear cub,
Swimming, shooting .22s,
Stringing bows, flinging arrows;
Eager to pick up stick and puck,
Play fifty "fast" games
Of box hockey on the Swamper Hill.
And, oh, how I loved eating sandwiches:
Egg salad, peanut butter and jelly,
Bologna and cheese, spam.

But when a man grows older,
His body draws up in size;
His eyes are dry even when he cries;
His reactions have a molasses flow,
And memory is a derelict auto.
Yet if he's lucky at all,
And just puts his mind to it,
He'll find the child he left behind,
Get back to the start before dark.
Being here today, I realize
I've arrived intact. Right now,
I could eat three desserts!

8/11/66

17

Keep the Fires Burning

For Larry Cartwright

When winter comes,
Who will hear the silent pines whining,
Grieving your absence
From this sacred land?
And which of you will still be listening
To the sandy, soft-trod paths
Pumiced under running feet?
Will the lake's prevailing breezes
That billowed spinnakers
Still fill sleep's retreats
When dreams won't sail an even course?

I know the answer to everything!
It's friendship, boys!
It wends through spruce and pine,
Insinuates lake waters,
Carves your faces on scrimshaw moons;
It sits beside you at dinner
And hides beneath your pillowed head.
Who can deny this precious essence,
Covenants made at season's end,
When snow and rain
Detain the slower spirit?

Today I'm witness to summer's grace.
You're the ones, boys! This is the place!
I beg you never to forget
This ritualed myth of immortality,
Your earthly birth
Here at Camp Nebagamon.
Being borne comes fast, sometimes.
Initiation is always swift.
For some, wisdom matures
In a youngster's mind,
While others take a lifetime to arrive.

Boys! Boys! This is the Truth!
Haven't you guessed yet?
Manhood is that ageless moment
When all else falls away
Except the promises you made
To stay in touch forever
With those who breathed and slept,
Ate and played and prayed with you.
You, boys, Tomorrow's men,
Will always be memory's mates
When you say the word *friend*,

And again and again,
"You're my *friend*!"

8/18/66

'Round Thy Blazing Council Fire's Light

Something mystic about singing together
Lifts a low-slung spirit;
It's the song sung from the heart
That pumps earth's lungs,
Fills the far-flung universe
With our collective voices
Echoing His original inspiration.

Tonight I hear His humming
Coming from the fire's tongues
And limb-tips of pine trees
Quivering in the breeze like a flutist's lips
Shaping melodies above his mouthpiece.
And I realize we're the Song we sing
Around the blazing fire of this sacred Council Ring.

8/18/66

Season's End

Trunks piled high like shipping crates
Outside dust-swirling cabins
Vacant as pepper tins
Await stevedores and porters
To load them onto freighters and trains
For destinations remote from this northern lake.

The boarded-up Rec' Hall
Doesn't reek of hot meals, hickory smoke,
Or feel the dizzy weight
Of campers milling, spilling milk
Off Lazy Susans onto hardwood floors
Sporting scars of two-score years.

The boys are heading slowly homeward
Down rusty, Soo Line tracks
Overgrown with grass,
Cracking barriers where birch ends
And the softer scents of poplar and ash
Are lost in diesel exhaust near Milwaukee.

We who waved at the Hawthorne depot,
Like trees shivering in winter,
Take to our private highways.
I and my rider, Emptiness,
Make hollow conversation,
Never get on a first-name basis.

But if Solitude has no easy solutions
For reversing the end of a season
Or returning surrendered freedom,
How can a mere human
Who's just bartered a lifetime in a day
Accept final departures gracefully?

Especially when he realizes
That the boys he's taught all summer,
And brought into their own,
Will never race down hills again
Where he'll still be waiting decades hence
To check their reckless descents.

8/19/66

From Many We Are One

Camp's final day,
Inundated with gray sighs,
Dawns in a slow-drizzle yawn.
Its raw, quick, cold, slick air
Keeps campers moving restlessly as emigrés
Passing through Ellis Island,
Repeating tedious farewells
To their two-month community.
It cramps my freedom-seeking spirit, too!

As visitor, I'm not quite outsider,
But friend among closer friends than I.
Despite long-standing affiliations,
My grief only approximates theirs.
Yet this is my home also,
A fifteen-year house of worship and play.
A lifetime in a day!
That's how it is with me
This Friday as I speculate on Fate.

Will I ever pass this way again,
Return to this place where overnight
Boys become men, men boys again
When days dwindle down in old age,
Extended winters come 'round
On a daily basis,
Burying beneath eight-foot snow drifts
Memory's golden tokens
Celebrating Youth's Olympians?

I shall return a few days each summer
As I have now at season's end
To retrieve those bright medallions
Glistening amidst pine needles and ferns:
Like phoenixes they'll rise from ashes
Of days and decades past,
Just as today, in the faces of these boys,
I see traces of their dads,
Cousins, uncles, nephews, and brothers;

Lads who through the whisperous years
Have not disappeared. Just as then,
Now I know what each of us found here
That brought us back, keeps us in touch,
Who'll never, never, never let go:
It's that legacy of friendship
Deeded us devotees
Charged with keeping the fires burning.
From many we are One: Camp Nebagamon!

8/19/66

To Duluth and Back

For Jane Jewell

Approaching this enchanted city
Asleep on a sloping hill
Like a cloaked, comatose princess
With a poison apple stuck in her throat,
We fear no necromantic filters,
Fully expect to be spelled
Just kneeling beside her,
Peering into her wide, open eyes.

Far out across Lake Superior,
Harbor beacons and channel markers,
Lorelei-sirens calling to sailors
On oarboats months at sea,
Recite erotic poetry:
Red, green, red, red, green,
Infinitely intermittent;
We listen to their distant glistening.

In Duluth, near St. Louis Bay,
By her pulp mills and railroad yards,
We park, embrace, gaze silently
At high-shouldered tankers
Being made sweet love to in their docks;
Going lower as their holds get filled
With Mesabi red and Prairie gold,
The world's most potent semen.

We retreat, stop to eat at a café
Just below Superior and Lake,
Savor a few zesty brews,
Buy a six-pack of Leinenkugel's
For our rendezvous with the moon,
Then drive up the North Shore
To a grot at water's edge
Where rocks give way to sandy beach.

Chilled by the swift, whipping wind,
We gather driftwood, sip beer,
Set a blaze, lie naked in its halo
On a blanket. With brazen impertinence
We dare Time to chase us,
Try to locate our hiding places
In Love's caves we explore.
She knows better than to disturb us!

Even as the bonfire dies,
Our heart-sparks brighten the darkness,
Guide us back to night's opening.
Entranced by those beacons and markers,
Grain elevators, oar docks,
Great Lakes tankers
Moored in that medieval port,
We drive to Nebagamon hallucinating,

Returning with the treasures of Youth
We'd discovered together in Duluth.
We knew they were there,
Just not where, 'til tonight
When we gently removed the apple
From her swollen throat, and she awoke.
Now, Prince and Princess kiss,
Slip happily ever after into History.

8/22/66

Counselors' Night Off

Silence rises from the mist.
Sibilant leaves in trees along the beach
Whisper secrets to the gibbous moon.
We eavesdrop on their gossiping
On the possibility we're being talked about.

Across Lake Nebagamon,
Past Honeymoon Point and the bay it guards
Like The Academy above the Hudson,
A shadow widens the void,
Screeches beneath the wind's raspy voice.

Is this Winter's premonitory plaint
Or just insistent fatigue
Pressing us forward toward restfulness?
Perhaps it's a heat lightning storm
Forming up in Ely or the Quetico.

No matter! Now is the hour
To suspend senses, head for our cabins,
Where campers in bunk beds drowse,
And surrender to three-blanket sleep:
Castle keepers for the next generation.

6/25/68

The Point

The long day lengthens out,
Drips pink inks
Into trees bordering Lake Nebagamon.
Sailboats buoyed in the sky
Miraculously come untied, tack
As navigators describe hieroglyphs
With their tillers, chart courses
Sailors from Tyre once plied.

Standing in sand on the Lumberjack Point,
A boy with hands in his pockets
Sings hymns to ancient winds.
His soft voice isn't lost
As it crosses waters beyond his vision.
Its echoes beckon him home.
Running wing and wing,
His dreams heel rapturously.

6/27/68

Pieces and Tatters

This place traces my mind's furrows,
Seeds and harvests me each summer,
And when I'm away
It haunts me nine months a day
Like the making of a child.

And now, God, and now,
I've returned to this sacred place
Where the air is decent for dreaming
And the moon has no lascivious thoughts.

I've come back to unloose myself,
Release a thousand balloons
Into the Milky Way
And watch them explode, drift down
As swallow, mayfly, and bat,
Scattering themselves like confetti
Above cabins where you boys stay.

I'm a ten-year-old again!
One of you, boys,
Re-teaching my eyes to dream
Before they speak, my tongue to see,
My soul to learn the poet's urge
To seize pieces and tatters of the world
And arrest them in patterns,
Just by being open to receive ecstasy
Whenever it screams to be seen, to be heard.

6/27/68

The Fishing Dock

Above the dock's rotted planks
I cease hearing echoes
Of reckless seconds passing me by.

Mayflies swarm in the warming air,
While fish at feeding,
Like seedlings
Breaking through to life,
Needle the lake's greenish patina.

Swallows follow the lowering sun;
Now twilight is shed
Of its red threads. Day is done!

Cabin lights
Across this diamond-flecked mirror
Float moons halfway to me:
Ring buoys into whose halos
I cast my eyes' lures.

6/27/68

Marianne

We drive a winding thread
From Minong to Hayward
Through birch, spruce, and pine trees,
Watching for red and green irridescences
Leaning towards our speed.
The moon is a spider
Caught in its own white web of clouds.

She flees Sweden, I, San Francisco,
Urgently;
We meet on foreign, neutral soil,
Beneath a circus tent,
Beside antique railroad sleeping cars:
Incest's identical twins
Reborne so far from our native hearts.

Diana seduces Apollo;
He follows her into the sky
Where deer suckle the stars
And the Northern Lights are in orgasm.
The web supporting us ripples
As we teeter at our wet lips' edges;
Yet its tenuous threads hold our weight.

A writer and a blond, long-haired,
Green-eyed Queen
Spin
        within
                night's vortex
Before crawling up inside the moon,
                        happily trapped!

8/8/68

Morning's Companion

Once more, for Jan

In my sandy bunk on this August morning,
While the sun's rotating color wheel
Buffs dawn's rough edges,
I feel my stiff body shifting,
And dry dreams drifting a few degrees.

Suddenly traces of a child's smile
Settle inside the tabernacle of my eyes;
I imagine you in bed beside me
As if we were cabin mates,
Not lovers separated for the summer.

The sweep second of sweet surprise
Erases all stations from Time's face
As, in a prophetic gesture of gentleness,
The future wife of a newer man
Completes the poet her slow kiss composes.

8/4/69

Interchanges

Cold wet weather,
Heavy as a dull crayon,
Colors Youth's eyes chipmunk auburn,
Pine-tree green;
It outlines them in spongy registers
Of punk and fungi, mold, mildew,
Mushroom, rust, and smut.
Knowing Nature, decay's mate,
Replaces what she undoes,
We set forth
Through this needle-silenced rain
To explore their friendless interchanges.

Approaching lush, hidden substances,
We grow eager to touch divinity,
Taste creation,
Watch God visible Himself.
Hush! Hush! I hear Him now
In this Wisconsin mist,
Whispering to us.

7/29/72

Prayer

For the generations of Camp Nebagamon

Three seasons have passed beneath my feet
Like separate choruses of an elegy
Composed for me. A leit motif
Recurring in each scheme and daydream,
Has touched a chord with sweet sympathies,

And I lean forward with all my weight
Pressed against the escape hatch. The latch
Gives easily. I course freely through night
Toward pinewhiney Wisconsin with my soul,
Spirit, and head totally out of control,

Ready to climb back out of Time's capsule
Onto your floating island. Take me in!
Let me renew my slow sunlit growth!
Make me an ornament in your gorgeous forest,
Suspended among unending memories and seeds

Recently planted! Cradle me in this retreat
Where boys become friends each summer,
And men spend entire adulthoods
Teaching Peaceable Kingdoms really exist!
Shake golden fruit from Wishing Trees

That I might taste Eden's delicacies,
Feed my imagination with enchanted fantasies!
In this sacred garden by Lake Nebagamon,
I feel safe, unafraid of expulsion,
A child again for the rest of my days.

7/30/72

33

Cabin by a Lake

The very notion of cliché
As a legacy of speech spoken or composed
Takes the form of a faint aroma
Emanating from a cabin at a boys' camp
Long ago outgrown by me
On a shore bordering a lake in northern Wisconsin
Lined with birch, poplar, and Norway pine.

It infiltrates my nose and eyes
As though I were fourteen again,
Lying on a bunk in Lumberjack Three
Reading *Moby Dick* or the "*Bounty*" trilogy.
For vague reasons, teacher,
I hear your seasoned voice urging me
To avoid employing clichéd phrases
And metaphors based on memories
Too subjectively conceived,
Or resorting to nostalgia and sentimentality,
Rather than inventing fresh analogies.

Today, despite your cautionary critiques,
That faint aroma of childhood chokes me.
Awakening from the present in panic,
I frantically reach up from my typewriter keys
To hold open a screen door
Flapping back and forth,
Like wings of a scavenging blackbird,
To keep it from closing forever
On a cabin bordering a lake in northern Wisconsin
I've been sleeping in each evening
These past twenty-three years.

6/23/74

Trial by Fire and Water*

As the past gathers momentum,
Vision blurs into a misty, reverse myopia
On whose unfocused lens memories converge.
Images splinter, accomplishments disintegrate
Like logs cast into a fireplace
And left overnight; I sweep up ashes
The years have created in their unclean burning.

Not even echoes of Youth's singing voices
Linger above regal Norway pines
Or between dense sumac and third-growth birch.
Nor do the sweet, adolescent faces
Beaming with promise, the athletic bodies
We boasted, the incomplete souls
Impatient to be molded into living shapes
Lifted from the rib of Michaelangelo's maker,
Swell with their original energy and purpose.

They've all become firebells on tripods
Caked with rust, cracked, without clappers;
Herb's whirligigs flaking mercilessly
In a vacuum where no winds stir;
Paddles, oars, and taut, billowed sails
Separated from their canoes, rowboats, yachts
Stranded on a lake drained of its waters.

I see screened, rough-framed cabins
Devoid of trunks, bunkbeds, laughter,
Inhabited instead by chipmunks and skunks.
Only their outlines highlighted by snow
And somber summer shadows
Locate them in the mind's mythical Wisconsin
My glowing spirit knew intimately
Before growing up and going away from home;
Even their green doors are warped shut.

My hands grope among cobwebs
Lining their rafters, dusty shelves, and ledges;
They stick to my fingertips like sadness.
I tug at what remains of frayed bell ropes;
The dull thud of bloodless years
Pulsates my brain. I spin thin propellers;
Ghosts see-saw in rickety imprecision.

I race along the lake's shore
Searching for washed-up shards of childhood,
Then skip deliriously over a liquidless surface
On golden stepping stones
Thrown across the water by a gibbous moon,
And follow its lunatic shimmering home.
But the path leads ever deeper
To the bottom of an empty crater. Still breathing,
I drown in its undertow.

1/5/79

*After reading the most recently received issue of the
Camp Nebagamon *Arrowhead,* the poet is overwhelmed
by a deathly premonition that he will never again be able to
recapture happy memories of his past, return to those
events and friendly faces comprising the chronicle of
seventeen summers spent at the boys' camp in northern
Wisconsin where he grew from adolescence into manhood.

Freedom Seeker

For my abiding friend, Buddy Herzog

At thirty-eight,
I've returned to Nebagamon's enchanted camp
Where icicle poplars, white birch,
Norway pine, and Douglas fir flourish,
Whose deep-green, conical designs
In this mystic Wisconsin
Define my spired reverence toward Nature.

I surrender my citified dissatisfactions
With happiness, forget my ambitions
And tendentious arguments.
The aroma of oak woodsmoke, scents of sumac,
Sap, and unpolluted lake water
Lifting into cool, blue evanescence
Unloose my spirit's inhibitions.

The exuberant child my heart outgrew
Re-emerges, first as shadow and breeze,
Then as bird, chipmunk, otter, and skunk,
Finally as chubby little boy-cub
Innocent of clichés and franchise mentalities,
Absolved of imperatives to measure up
Financially.

As I sit listening to the sky speak,
Youth's omniscient ignorance and sweet naiveté
Tempt me with heady desires to retreat,
Retire to this sylvan wilderness
For the remainder of my ordained life,
Become poet of pine needles and crickets,
Fate's surrogate Recorder of Deeds.

But Reality conspires against my lark.
It's just too far to travel
To get back to the start before dark.
Instead, I pen this gentle lament
For my children to sing to their offspring
When God quits whispering in my ears:
It's the closest thing to freedom I'll ever achieve.

8/19/79

37

Of Fishes and Bears

For Max J. Lorber,
"Muggs,"
The Bull of the Woods
1902-1982

So distant this moment
From the Wisconsin of my summertide
Where his manly, full-flowering spelled me,
Yet so close now that I know
He has departed; I grow serene,
Draw nearer his gone spirit
As memories call me home.

I'm alone again, a boy of ten,
A lost, awkward, chubby bear cub
Scurrying nervously over sandy paths
Birch-dappled, tangled in ferns and sumac,
Searching for his familiar voice
Echoing yet from the "Big House" hill,
Still filling the Rec' Hall with anthems;

A cub wading Lake Nebagamon,
Tonguing its ripples to slake my thirst,
Hoping to see Muggs breach, expunge silence
In the shape of a muskellunge
Arrested forever in the dripping sunset's net,
Trying, even in death, to out-best perfection;
That gesture, his epitaph and apogee!

3/17/82

Obsession

I leave home at 5:55.
Everywhere, low-lying mists
Slither and hiss through twisted grass
Like vipers in a fiery forest.

Sun and moon, Capulet and Montague
Chasing each other across catwalks
Bracing the sky's theater,
Pantomime destiny's daily acts

I've tried two decades to unmemorize,
Even rewrite occasionally.
They remind me reason
Yet feuds with its foe, emotion.

How, after so many uprootings,
Solitude and loneliness still hold sway
Over encroaching lunacy
Is an enigma metaphor can't explain.

I know only that this latest trip
From Farmington to northern Wisconsin
Started before my heart's first stirring,
And not even Death can abort it.

7/1/83

You Can't Go Back, Exactly

For Frank Sachs

A slightly different rite,
This flight to Wisconsin's northern reaches;
Being met at the Duluth airport
And chauffeured through Superior southeast
Past unincorporated Wentworth, Poplar,
Down county trunk "P"
To the Village of Lake Nebagamon,
Then into the boys' camp.
Arriving so swiftly from door to door,
I'm dizzied; the mystic distance
Is so much shorter than I remember it being
When the boy in me made his odysseys,

Departing Union Station in St. Louis
On the Gulf, Mobile & Ohio's
All-aluminum, red and maroon diesels
Shuttling up the Prairie past Springfield,
Bloomington, Joliet,
On into Chicago's La Salle Street depot;
Being taxied en masse by Parmalee cab
Across town to Dearborn Station
Where we ate at Fred Harvey's Restaurant
Before boarding a Soo Line charter's
World War II Pullman cars
For the all-night run to Hawthorne junction:

Playing cards in hot drawing rooms,
Traipsing aisles single file,
Heaving water balloons like grenades
Between berth curtains,
Leaning out the open upper half
Of a drafty vestibule door,
Absorbing whiffs of gritty coal smoke
Issuing from the chuffing stack
Of History's last active steam locomotive,
Being lullabied to sleep
By the rhythmic clack-clacking of steel wheels
Playing taps over unbutted tracks.

40

Returning to Camp Nebagamon
Twenty-five years later,
I make the same trek, almost.
Not as a boy, but writer of verse
Invited to "Explore Creativity"
For camp's "Trails Forward" program,
I measure with metaphor and rhyme-chime
Vast contrasts between jet travel,
With its fast, absolute precision,
And the exasperating unpredictability
Of interminable trips by passenger train
We reveled in during the fifties

When still we could weave through cities
Shimmering on midnight's fringes,
Snake past factories, ghettos, tenements,
See inside lighted houses
Moving human shapes, and invent
Lives desperately quiet
Or spent in opulence on the diorama
Spinning just inches behind the window
To which we kept noses and lips pressed
In ecstasy lasting the night,
Listening to the intermittent whistle
Get all mixed up in our dreams

When we still believed that if we wished,
Like Huck Finn and the Sawyer kid,
We could sneak off the train
At the very next station,
Light out for the territories
Beyond the Dakotas, Wisconsin, Minnesota,
Hiking all the way to the horizon;
Maybe spend the rest of our days
Rafting the entire River;
Certainly not worry about being hijacked,
Crashing from 37,000 feet,
Or arriving five minutes ahead of schedule!   41

7/1/83

Rites of Way

Now, my six-day escape
To Wisconsin's North Woods
Fades into shade, shape,
Scent of Norway pine,
Diminishes to brain-saturation
Faint, yet crisp.
Memory and forgetting
Vie for priority
In my lapsing imagination.

But Camp Nebagamon's
Immemorial magic —
Its chipmunks, cabins, canoes,
And campers — continues to grow.
At forest's edge
A boy emerges,
Waves to his aging shadow
Portaging home,
Then re-enters the woods alone.

7/6/83

Tone Poem for Two Voices*

Troika: From up here all the
clouds look like pebbles
in a stream.

Right now I feel
like I could go skipping
over them

Dad: and get from one side
of the universe
to the other.

6/26/88

* Composed responsively by the poet and his son while
in flight to Camp Nebagamon.

Walt Whitman in the Land
of Paul Bunyan

As if sporting Walt Whitman's aura,
I've traipsed here and yon
This entire dappled Wisconsin afternoon
Over all 67 acres
Of sand-strewn pine, sumac, and birch stands
Nestling Lake Nebagamon.
I've celebrated each atom of this sacred place,
Every pine needle and pendant raspberry,
Praised with silent incantations
The magic that has transformed generations of boys
Into men two months each summer
For the last sixty years.

I've paused just long enough to revel
In the chipmunk's mixture of spots and stripes,
The birch tree's curious parchment bark,
Lose myself in daydreamy meditation
On a splintery bench in the Council Ring,
Hoping to hear the totem pole,
Carved in 1936,
Tell tales told long ago,
Sing songs sung in swaying fellowship
Whose faded lyrics, even in this moment,
Strain to reconnect with echoing refrains
Memory hums from its own collective memory.

I've come all this way alone,
Strayed from commoner pursuits to seek truth,
Knowing my ambitiousness borders on hubris,
Augers poorly for discovering solutions
Or even drawing finite conclusions
To ultimate considerations of human lifespan,
Last rites, and final disposition of ashes.
And yet, with a quixotic wrist-flick of the dice
I've risked all possible misfortune
On the vaguest chance
That by returning to this Arcadian haunt
Where I grew two decades beyond puberty,

I just might uncover the "why?" in the road
Where the veering first occurred,
My psyche began searching for words instead of persons
As instruments for expressing innermost emotions,
Dreams, revelations, cosmic visions.
But the supple, sweet faces I've seen today
Playing in pure male camaraderie
Shame my investigations; painfully they remind me
I'm a priest without a parish,
And that defining Truth, birthing verse
Are not worthy substitutes
For repopulating the earth with progeny.

6/26/88

Accompanying My Son to Summer Camp

The uninterpretable recitation of psalms
By birds, chipmunks, and breezes
Playing hide and seek in the reaches
Of birch, poplar, Norway pine,
Transpose earth, lake, and sky into verse.
They create a majestical electricity
That reverberates Youth's ears
With faded measures and cadences,
Resurrects the eyes with their reflections.
An almost verbal quality of light
Sifting through this Wisconsin latitude
Speaks oracularly about my future,
Catapults me in a swirl of reveries
Backward into my unfolding past
As if asleep in a waking hallucination.

Seated beneath these pines,
A man in a boys' outdoor shrine,
Reluctantly delivering up his son
To summer camp for two months,
I realize how Time translates itself
Across the generations of man
Without ever catching up with its echo
Or questioning the uniqueness of its repetitions.
The simple verities are imperishable!
But right now, my boy and I
Are too absorbed in exploring and recording
Wind-stir and bird-chirping
For me to notice nature's Book
Contains the same words and phrases
The Lord spoke to Abraham about Isaac.

6/26/88

C.N.O.C.*

For Will Fisher

In this pine-and birch-bowered grot
Whose turf, like the back of an aged hand,
Shows its veins and roots,
Fires made from kindling shaved from logs
Meticulously chopped with hatchets
By guildsmen learning Nature's trades,
Blaze proudly, warming earth's halo.
Nearby, others practice knot-tying,
(Clove hitch, Bowline on a bite,
Lark's head, Sheetbend, Square, and Clinch),
While a few remove a Catskill from its cocoon,
Begin smoothing stitched sheets,
Fitting aluminum tubular poles,
The whole ballooning in a fell swoop,
Like a sail raised up a ship's mast,
Until it stands formidable in its fragility,
Able to withstand a Kansas cyclone.

Then the apprentices begin their dismantling;
Magically the tent collapses back
Into its protective sack,
As if even for a matter of precious seconds
It hadn't embodied majesty;
As if the boys never had arrived
At this sanctuary beneath the pines
To practice life-skills in preparation
For overnighters across the decades;
As if the years themselves did not exist
Except as messengers of essences
For potential listeners and lookers to possess,
Who, by providence or design
On such a glorious morning, might desire
To conspire in recreating the Universe
By witnessing a group of rag-tag campers
Discover how a few of earth's miracles work.

6/27/88

* Camp Nebagamon Outing Club

Morning Ritual

For Nardie and Sally,
with my love

They awaken beneath hand-me-down blankets
From fifty-degree northern Wisconsin sleep
In shabby, screened-in cabins,
Emerge into the morning through a yawn,
Struggle down or up paths —
There is absolutely no level turf here —
Toward the Rec' Hall in jeans,
Flannel shirts, floppy tennis shoes,
Congregate at the Axman and LJ porches
Waiting for Paul Bunyan's shofar to blow,
Call them to repast; they enter
In disorderly droves, home-in on tables
Whose Lazy Susans are crowded with cereals,
French toast, milk cartons, bowls,
Wait again for the "Day Push"
To read from a 3 x 5 card
Morning's sermonette: "When given lemons,
Make lemonade......Be seated."
They eat noisily; K.P.s retrieve "seconds"
As each boy discusses what activities
He might sign up for with his buddies.

Breaking fast in this sacred hive
Is a ritual shared by excited little lives
Shimmering with ambitions and goals
Corrected not to unspecified time
But set for "right now,"
Immediately after cabin clean-up
When they'll rush off to Air Riflery,

***

Canoeing, Craft Shop,
C.N.O.C. to chop logs,
Pitch tents, tie knots, boil water
In unlacquered, #10 tin cans,
Cook over a grate, bake pies and cakes
In aluminum reflector ovens;
These precocious faces
Sccdcd with slowly-unfolding blooms
Growing one smile, one joke at a time,
Who know not the waste of adult distractions
And dalliances, care only about the moment,
As indeed they should!,
Approach each new day with a magician's focus
On the hat hopefully containing a rabbit
They're certain will materialize
If only they recite the appropriate hocus-pocus:
"I *can* do it.....I *know* I can!"

And so they grow, going through splendid motions
Recalling butterflies from caterpillars,
Themselves fluttering up, hovering,
Soaring above the rim of brimless hats
Their imaginations wear and change
Ten times daily during adolescence.
Bless the children! These prescient faces
Contain the coded keys to Rosetta stones
We don't even suspect
Lay buried just up ahead
In the rubble of as yet unconstructed Acropolises,
Ninevahs, and Carcassonnes.
Bless each child individually
For his unique conception,
And collectively in their reckless ecstasy.

6/27/88   49

From the Corner of Main Street and Lake Avenue, Lake Nebagamon, Wisconsin

From where I bear witness to this street scene
Comprising Lake Nebagamon's entire downtown,
I can see in a single sweep
The "Lawn Beach Inn,"
Malinowski's false-front, all-purpose store,
Finell's and Bridge's bars, Dairy Queen,
The dentist's office, boarded-up Standard station,
And rust-colored, log Auditorium
Overlooking the municipal dock and "swimming hole."

This restaurant with its 50s motel decor
(High gloss white pine panelling,
Chromolitho of Christ staring skyward
With uncompromising vacancy in his eyes)
Is a newcomer to this Lilliputian community,
Which explains why it retains a semblance
Of 'a clean, well-lighted place'
Into whose quietude I've committed myself,
A wayfarer seeking a home-cooked meal.

Although night hasn't overtaken twilight,
Each vehicle maneuvering down Lake Avenue
Uses headlights. Couples strolling,
Holding hands or ice cream cones,
Echoing friendly overtures, gentle gestures
From Winslow Homer watercolors,
Bend and sway in pantomimic motion,
Croon refrains from tunes
End-rhyming in "moon," "June," and "loon."

This derelict lumber town
Is a railroad hobbiest's scaled-down model
Whose twelve-year heyday
Commenced in 1898
When the Weyerhaeusers set up their mill,
Built a summer "Big House" on the hill
And proceeded to denude the land of its timber
With oblivious disregard for 1910
When every last Truffula tree would be cut.

Today, only a few year-round residents,
A hardy, if almost non-extant, enclave
Persist in this precarious habitat
Whose ecology remains curiously stable.
Perhaps it's the Fitgers and Hamms in their blood
Or Scandinavian accents on their tongues
That keep the population from deviating
More than a score either way every decade.
Tonight I celebrate each of Lake Nebagamon's

564 souls
Recorded on its voting rolls. I, a wayfarer
Returning to my birthplace
To assess our desolation,
Have come home to pay last respects
Before heading out from Superior or Duluth
Aboard America's last passenger train
Running south. In a few hours
My childhood will be a thing of the past, again.

6/27/88

A Grieving Rain

Let this soft mouth, shapèd to the rain
Be but golden grief for grieving's sake,
And these green woods be dreaming here to wake
Within my heart when I return again.

"Mississippi Hills: My Epitaph"
William Faulkner

Returning without my youthful companion,
Whom I'd accompanied to camp
Thirty miles southeast of Duluth,
I ruminate on this rainy a.m.
Still seeping into forgetting's turf.
Even now, flying toward St. Louis,
My dry feet keep getting wet
As I try to avoid stepping in puddles
Collecting between exposed root clusters
Of majestic Norway pines
And at the base of railroad-tied terraces
Leading from Swamper Hill
To the Rec' Hall where a blazing fire
Vigils 7:30 breakfast.

Now, as then, my toes and leg bones
Retain a vague chill,
As if the letting go has not been accomplished
Without Nature exacting retribution
For my having left in her keeping
An adventitious responsibility,
My ten-year-old son, Troika.
Nor can I completely jettison
My sense of emptiness deserting him
In that upper bunk, under three blankets,
After rousing him from a tranquil drowse
Just long enough to kiss his lips
And listen to him mumble a wish,
"Tell Mom and Tril I love and miss them."

Although so alone soaring home,
Chastizing myself for having sacrificed him,
I celebrate his rite of passage,
Assume intuition has presumed correctly
For my child's evolving future.
After all, self-reliance *is* a solitary pursuit,
Rarely convenient or reassuring.
Nevertheless, my regret is like the rain:
Its wetness penetrates memory,
Gets into my eyes and settles there
Like puddles I keep stepping in, sloshing through,
Between exposed root clusters of Norway pines,
Day after summer day,
Waiting for my boy to return.

6/28/88

Male Bonding

Even though I've been home three days,
A persistent image of you and me
Investigating the camp grounds,
Climbing hills, following sandy paths,
Sharing a session at Air Riflery,
A chair at your table in the Rec' Hall,
Continues projecting from an endless reel
As though memory were a theater screen
On which we see our selves
Fixed in a dream sequence.
In this artificial light
Flickering through the distance dividing us,
Not by seventy-two hours
Or the ineffable silence that widens daily
As summer reaches eight weeks out,
But by thirty-seven years,
I realize my participation is vicarious,
Not visceral; our existence volitional.

Nonetheless, my blessed, precious son,
Mark this well! For a father and his boy,
Joy is a felt experience when both
Can focus from separate heights
And superimpose facsimile images;
Just as you, lying prone on a mat,
Aiming that wavering Daisy rifle,
And I, sitting behind you on a bench,
Simultaneously knew
Each time you hit the bullseye
Or perforated the target's white periphery

***

Fifteen feet away. It's amazing
How I could feel the energy you applied,
My boy, squeezing that trigger:
The first finger on my right hand
Neither atop nor beneath yours,
But rather inside it, like identical twins
Owing allegiance to their common cell.

6/30/88

The Fountain of Youth

For my blessed boy, Troika,
with Dad's deep love

All Thursday and Friday, my boy and I
Have shared gentle camaraderie,
Keeping the goodbye hour
From sneaking up on us without warning
Like it did five weeks ago.
We've tried to find a happy medium
Between our mean ages,
Disentangle yesterday from today,

And reduce our differences in temperament
To the lowest common denominator:
Camp Nebagamon.
Holding hands this last evening,
We descend Swamper Hill,
Inspired by the sweet, thick scent of pine,
The hush of moist shadows after rain.
Troika walks in its drainage ruts

As if seeking his own level.
I follow at his side; he guides me
Past the shrine. Reaching the Axman Village
We head left, down to the lake,
Along the road running behind cabins
Astir with Lumberjack laughter.
Finally we arrive at water's edge;
Boy and dad, entranced by its tranquility.

Although the moon is conspicuously missing,
Vision is unaffected;
We see whatever our eyes touch,
Like a blind man tapping his cane tip
As he negotiates a congested street:
Houses rimming the shore, trees, bats,
Fish breaching the surface for insects.
We fathom our inner happiness;

It leads us up the hill again
To the Swamper Village; a glowing halo
Showing us paths through the darkness.
It's the circle through camp we've completed,
But also something else:
A transcendence we've achieved,
Who at ten and forty-seven
Have entered Love's orbit soaring.

Taps softly awakens us from our senses,
Commends us to its benediction.
We hug the breath out of each other,
Kiss lips, cheeks, forehead
Like all our ancestors have done.
Troika says, but only once,
"Please, won't you please stay?"
"You know I can't, Mr. Boy."

Hand on the screen door, he pauses, turns,
Squeezes me again, then disappears.
Before slipping out of his Village, I stoop
For the first time in thirty-five years
To sip from the fountain of youth
At which Troika and his mates drink daily.
Instantaneously, its bracing, egg-taste
Reclaims me, and I know I won't ever go.

7/30/88

LOUIS DANIEL BRODSKY

Louis Daniel Brodsky was born in St. Louis, Missouri, in 1941, where he attended St. Louis Country Day School. After earning a B.A., Magna Cum Laude, at Yale University in 1963, he received an M.A. in English from Washington University in 1967 and an M.A. in Creative Writing from San Francisco State University in 1968.

Mr. Brodsky is the author of fourteen volumes of poetry as well as nine scholarly books on Nobel laureate William Faulkner. Listing his occupation as Poet, he is also an adjunct instructor at Mineral Area College in Flat River, Missouri, Curator of the Brodsky Faulkner Collection at Southeast Missouri State University in Cape Girardeau, Missouri, and President of Timeless Press, Inc., St. Louis.

With his wife Jan, daughter Trilogy, and son Troika, he lives in St. Louis, Missouri.